Romeo Cianchetta

ASSISI
Art and History
in the Centuries

CENTRO STAMPA EDITORIALE
plurigraf
PERSEUS

Index

Introduction 5

Basilica of St. Francis 9

    Lower Church 19

    Upper Church 42

    The giottesque sequence of the life of St. Francis 52

Inside the City 74

Piazza del Comune 78

Chiesa Nuova and Oratory of S. Francesco Piccolino 80

S. Francesco Piccolino 80

Cathedral of St. Ruphinus 82

Rocca Maggiore 88

Basilica of St. Clare 92

Abbey Church of St. Peter 97

Outskirts of Assisi: Church of San Damiano 98

Church of San Damiano 98

Hermitage of the Prisons 101

Feasts and traditions of Assisi 104

Santa Maria degli Angeli 113

Basilica of Santa Maria degli Angeli 113

Church of Santa Maria di Rivotorto 123

Chapel of Satriano 124

Canticle of the Creatures 125

Plan of Town 126

Revision: Anna Caprespa

Photographs: Archivio Plurigraf - Scala - Vescovo
               The air photographs have been authorized by S.M.A.
               permission n.506 - 20th June,1991

© Copyright
CASA EDITRICE PERSEUS - PLURIGRAF collection
Published and printed by Centro Stampa Editoriale, Sesto Fiorentino, (Fi).

«*Having returned from Spoleto to Assisi, one day he went out into the country to meditate, and found himself near the little Church of San Damiano, which was threatened by the ruin of age. Inspired by God, he entered the Church and, at the feet of the Crucifix, praying with great fervor, he felt his soul fill with joy. Then he raised up his tearful eyes, and he heard in his ear a mysterious voice. That voice came down from the lips of the crucified Christ, and was addressed to himself. Three times it repeated. "Francis, restore my house that, as you see, is falling into ruin"*».

Plurigraf Publishing aims with this publication to commemorate the events of the earthquake which struck the Marche and our own Region of Umbria, on 26th September 1997. Commemoration of this event is in fact a way of expressing a homage to the sorrow of a whole population and regret for the harm done to many monuments.
In particular, this book is intended to stand as a witness to what happened.

Introduction

…sisi (Asisium to the Romans, …cesi in the Middle Ages) lies in …ntral Umbria, bordered by Peru-…a, Gualdo Tadino, Nocera, Foli-…o, Spello, Bettona, Bastia Umbra; …rough it run the rivers Chiascio …d Topino. The township covers …out 18,000 hectares. The town is …ilt on the western flank of majestic …unt Subasio, bounded on the …rth by the deep gorge dug by the …rent Tescio, and on the south by …e splendid Umbrian plain.

…hat were its origins? In prehistory …was a village of one of the most …cient of the Italic peoples, the …bri, who lived about the time of …e so-called Villanovan civilization. …m that epoch very little has come …wn to us: simple terracotta, or …ttery, urns, stone and bronze …owheads. Later it underwent the …ilizing influence of the more …hly developed Etruscans, after

they established themselves on the right side of the Tiber, constituting the nearby «Lucumonia» (an Etruscan designation of a territory controlled by a chief called "Lucumo") of Perugia.

This is the historical reality, though a legend (one common to many other cities in search of noble origins), would have Assisi founded by the Trojan prince Asio (from which the name Sub-Asio, i.e., «under Asio's rule» would have been derived).

After the Battle of Sentino (295 B. C.), which marked the final defeat of the Etruscan and Umbrian coalition against Rome, Assisi fell under Roman rule, and was made a «municipium», with the duty of providing soldiers for the legions, but benefitting from the economic and civil rights of Roman citizens. Its flourishing economic position and the efficiency of its autonomous civil structure are

attested to by the Forum (under the present Town Hall Square), by the Temple of Minerva, by the remains of an amphitheatre and of Public Baths.

Christianity spread quickly there, and found its martyr in Bishop Rufino, who preached the Gospel in the first half of the third century. After the fall of the Roman Empire, Assisi, too, underwent the violence of barbarian invasions, and was partially destroyed by Totila's Goths in 505 A. D.

After a brief subjection to the Eastern Roman Empire, it went to the Longobards of the nearby duchy of Spoleto.

In the eleventh century Assisi entered the avant-garde of the movement against feudalism, in quest of the liberties of the city-state: in this connection there is a famous edict of this town whereby freedom

was given to land serfs who, in fleeing the rule of the feudal lord, would take refuge within its walls.

In the twelfth century it became fiercely Ghibelline and it housed an imperial garrison, which was driven out by a popular uprising in reaction to the abuse of power by Duke Conrad of Uslingen, Lieutenant of the Emperor Frederick I, called Barbarossa (Redbeard) around 1198.

In the thirteenth and fourteenth centuries it fought Guelph Perugia: in one of the many battles in 1202, at Collestrada, the Perugians took young Francis prisoner.

During those two centuries, notwithstanding so much internal and external strife, Assisi built its stupendous churches, its austere public buildings, its towers and walls, bringing in the most famous architects and painters for the purpose.

Great shrewdness was shown in the administration of the public goods. The town became rich through profitable commerce; art and trades were regulated through powerful guilds. With the terrible sacking by Piccinino (1442), a ferocious soldier of fortune, the decline of Assisi begins.

After long and bitter family feuds between the Nepis and the Fiumi, the city at the beginning of the sixteenth century becomes part of the temporal domain of the Church. Under the Popes it finds peace, but the atmosphere is dull and exhausted, very far from the creative fervor generated by the municipal liberties. In 1860, in a unanimous plebiscite, crowning the Italian Risorgimento, to which great citizens contributed generously, Assisi binds its destiny to that of the new Italy. On the occasion of the celebration of the seventh centenary of St. Francis' death (1926-27), Assisi once again drew to itself the attention of the world of religion and culture, thanks also to the fervor of the Franciscan family and to the works of some great writers, among them Paul Sabatier, Arnaldo Fortini, Johannes Joergensen, and Father G. Abate.

It is also interesting that Assisi was the first town to be visited by the Popes, after the so-called voluntary confinement which followed the end of the Papal States: on the 4th of October, 1962, Pope John XXIII made a pilgrimage to the tomb of St. Francis, who had been proclaimed Patron of Italy by his predecessor, Pius XII (June 18, 1939). The words spoken by Pope John in the Basilica of St. Francis will remain indelible in the history of Franciscanism and of Assisi.

«... O holy town of Assisi, you are known to the whole world for the o. fact of having given birth to the Lit. Poor One, your Saint, so seraphic his love. May you understand th privilege, and offer to all people t spectacle of such a faithfulness Christian tradition that it will be your real and everlasting honour.

... Here, with Saint Francis, here t are truly at the gates of Paradise.

... The moderate and wise use of t

utiful and good things that Province has distributed to the world, including no one, useful to all, is *aven on earth. We ask ourselves: y did God give Assisi this enchant-nt of nature, this aura of sanctity, most suspended in the air, which pilgrim almost tangibly feels? The swer is simple. So that men, ough a common and universal guage, will learn to recognize the* Creator, and to recognize each other as brothers».

The view of Assisi from the south or from the west, where the main roads enter, is spendidly picturesque: one cannot fail to stop for a while just to look, so great is its appeal. The visitor will leave with an indelible memory, one that will make him always want to come back to Assisi again. It is a mediaeval town, built on the western spur of Mount Subasio, lengthwise from southwest to northeast, in layered terraces.

Above it, in the center, alone and dominant, is the Rocca Maggiore (506 m. above sea-level).

The structure of the town would fall into the usual scheme of mediaeval urban planning, dictated by defense needs, were it not for the Basilica of St. Francis and the sacred monastery

girdling it, on the outermost western limits of the town. This is an imposing mass, characterized by powerful buttresses, by a double succession of very high arches, by a warm rosy-white colour, with a patina of old gold, which is enhanced by the clear blue of the Umbrian sky.

Its architectural structures, the elegant and peculiar movement of the masses, give the whole complex a symbolic value: that of an un-shakeable fortress of faith.

In the illustrations on the first pages we have shown fragmentary views of Assisi, seen from different angles, so as to bring out the principal characteristics of the town and its landscape values.

We have tried to fit into the frame the two main supports of Assisi's landscape: Mount Subasio and the Umbrian plain.

Without these, which make a poetic comment, we would never understand the Franciscan message which emanates from Assisi.

BIOGRAPHICAL SKETCH OF THE LIFE OF ST. FRANCIS, FROM HIS BIRTH (1181-82) UNTIL 1206

In order to avoid repetitions, we shall follow the Saint's life, from 1206 until his death in 1226, in the commentary on Giotto's cycle of frescoes in the Upper Church of the Basilica.

On an uncertain date, sometime between September, 1181, and February, 1182 Francis was born in Assisi to Pietro di Bernardone and Madonna Pica.

The father was a rich cloth merchant, a member of that growing bourgeoisie through which civil liberties were won, in contrast with the landed nobility who wanted to preserve their feudal privileges.

His mother was the Madonna Pica, a Provençal lady whom Pietro di Bernardone had married during one of the business trips he often took to France. The name «Francis» was given to him by his father (his mother had had him baptized John (Giovanni), during one of Pietro di Bernardone's frequent absences),

with the express intention of paying homage to the land of France, which had so enriched him.

Francis' formation was very much influenced by his mother, especially his chivalrous conception of life: a conception we often find in his actions and ideas, for example, that of his mystical wedding to the Lady Poverty. From his mother he learned the language of the troubadours, and he used it in his moments of poetic inspiration, both before and after his conversion.

He received the usual education of young gentlemen of his time: he learned Latin and calculus under the guidance of the priests of the Church of S. Giorgio (now the Chapel of the Basilica of S. Chiara). While still an adolescent, he was set to work in his father's cloth shop, successfully, it seems. Young Francis, well-provided with means and with intelligence, of an open character (today we would say extraverted), vain, expensively dressed, generous, became by unanimous consent the «prince» of the young set in Assisi. First in festivities, first in poetry contests, first in all activities of Assisi's youthful crowd of the time, he thought as well of excelling in arms, of becoming a knight. Contrary to what his carefree life might suggest, his manner was extremely kind, affable, well-spoken, an enemy to vulgarity, and exemplary in his relationships with women. And he was always kind and generous with the poor.

His first biographer, Tommaso da Celano, says that:

«... the beauty of the fields, the enchantment of vineyards, all that was pleasing to the eye, filled him with joy».

This sort of sentiment was almost unknown among men of his time.

In 1202, fulfilling his obligations as a citizen, in defending his city at war with Perugia, he was taken prisoner at Collestrada, near Ponte S. Giovanni.

He regained his freedom in 1203, following a peace treaty.

Back in Assisi, he resumed, perhaps even more intensely, his former way of life, until, at the age of twenty-three, he fell so seriously ill that his life was in danger for some time.

Slowly regaining his heath, he w back to his mundane life, but with enthusiasm, and with a vague a ety in his soul. His dream of bec ing a knight seemed on the poin realization when he decided to in Puglia Count Gualtieri III Brienne, who was fighting to b back to the usurped Principality Taranto the legitimate heir of Normans, the Empress Consta widow of Henry IV.

He acquired for himself and companion, noble but poor, all rich equipment necessary, and for Spoleto, the first stage on his to Puglia.

In Spoleto, however, he fell ill, an moment of high fever, he heard voice of the Lord, calling him to service: «*Go back to your city; th you will be told what to do*». Bac Assisi again, he was no longer a attracted by worldly life, but meditation and prayer: he found ideal refuge in the caves near Assi In 1206, in the crumbling l Church of San Damiano, while pr ing before the Crucifix, the sa voice he heard in Spoleto now g him his orders: «*Go, Francis, rest my house, which, as you can see falling into ruin*». It was a symbo order, entrusting Francis with a v high duty: that of restoring the div principles of Christ's Church, thre ened by heresy, by immorality, simony. Francis couldn't then und stand the hidden meaning, but c the literal one.

So he began, with the enthusia characteristic of him, to restore little Church materially. To find necessary means to do it, he so number of bolts of precious cloth Foligno. taken from his fath stores, and his own horse as well. father, already vexed by the mark changes in Francis' life, and dis pointed in the great ambitions he nurtured for his son, become inf ated and requested the Town Ma trates to take official note of intention to disinherit him, and banish him from the town county. The Consols could not in vene in the case, perhaps beca Francis had already taken mi Orders, and they transferred the c to the Bishop of Assisi.

asilica of St. Francis

rk on the construction of the Basilica of St. Francis began in 1128, only two years after the th of the Saint. The rocky terrain, overlooking the valley of the Tescio on the north, and the brian plain on the south, was given to the Order of Friars Minor by some rich citizens of Assisi, transcribed as property, to Pope Gregory IX, in deference to the Franciscan Rule, which erely forbade the acceptance under that title. From this Notary's deed derives the fact that the ilica and the Convent are still part of the patrimony of the Vatican.

place was formerly called the «Hill of Hell», because death sentences had been carried out e; but now it became «Paradise Hill», because it was to preserve through the centuries the tal remains of St. Francis. We do not know who the architect was: probably it was the General ister of the Order, Friar Elia of Bombarone.

great, and much-renowned, energy of Friar Elia, the enthusiasm of the workmen, and the ve participation of the people of Assisi, made it possible for the Lower Church to be pleted in only two years. On the 25th of May, 1230, the body of the Saint was brought there, n its temporary burial place in the Church of S. Giorgio.

speed with which the work was conducted surprises: it is doubtful that it could be done y, though we have technical means that are so much more advanced. Only the meeting of and faith could produce such a miracle!

Basilica of St. Francis - Panorama.

One reaches the Lower Square of the Basilica of St. Francis by passing through an arch at the end of the narrow Via Frate Elia.

We are suddenly faced with a stupendous view of the Basilica: on each side of the Square are the arcades of the wide piazza, which, in their play of perspectives, seem to indicate to us the destination of our steps, with an invitation to visit. In the center is the Romanesque bell-tower, the vestibule of the entry; above, to the right, the façade of the Upper Church. The rosy-white stone of Subasio, with which the Church was built, creates a particular chromatic effect, of great pictorial beauty. Through a twin portico in Gothic style, with in its center a finely carved rose, the work of Francesco of Pietrasanta (end of the XV century), one enters the Lower Church. The plan of the Church is a double T (the *Tau* so dear to Francis because it symbolizes the Cross).

Basilica of St. Francis.

CHAPEL OF ST. MARTIN

(first Chapel to the left of the nave).

ft-hand page:
above:
*The double
portal at the
itrance of the
ower Church.*

Below:
*The old
cemetery
(XV c.).*

On this page:
*The Chapel of
St. Martin
frescoed by
ione Martini.*

The Chapel dedicated to St. Martin was decorated with glass windows and frescoes by Simone Martini, around 1317, by commission of Cardinal Gentile di Partinico da Montefiore, a Franciscan Friar Minor, who had been an Apostolic Delegate on important diplomatic missions many times and who, though he died before that year, had left a conspicuous legacy for the completion of the work. The coat of arms of the Cardinal is repeated a number of times in the frescoes and in the decoration. The frescoes were revalued and almost rediscovered, by modern scholarly criticism, and they have an important place in the history of XIV c. art. They are the result of the meeting and confrontation of the Sienese School and the Florentine School. In Simone Martini the characteristics of the Sienese School, remain alive: the sweet mysticism, the purity of line, the refined colours, the rhythm in the design; but one immediately feels that direct contact with Giotto's painting, particularly that of the Upper Church, had a strong influence on him.

Plasticity and space enter his compositions. His art is enriched by the positive consistency of the third dimension, to be perceived both in the setting of the scene and in the figures. Another result of this meeting is a more luminous colour, one richer in light and shadow, more suggestive. The meeting of the two Schools to be seen in Simone Martini was to constitute a point of departure for the subsequent evolution of Italian painting. But in its renewed form, Martini remains far from Giotto's dramatic force, and continues to treat the aristocratic themes of chivalric ideals with delicate refinement.

Chapel of St. Martin: Detail of the Death of St. Martin (Simone Martini)
The Dream of St. Martin (Simone Martini). St. Martin Divides His Cloak with a Beggar.

hapel of St. Martin: St. Martin renounces his military career (Simone Martini).

Lower Church: Stained glass of the Chapel of St. Catherine or Chapel of the Crucifix - Detail (Giovanni di Bonino).

ter recent cleaning, which took
way a thick layer of dust, accum-
ated in the course of centuries,
ere reappeared the first frescoes of
e Basilica, attributed by some to
unta Pisano or to one of his
llowers.
nce this authority is very uncertain,

it was agreed to attribute the work to
an artist not better identified than by
the name of Master of St. Francis.
The sequence of frescoes was mutilated by the opening of the arches
leading to the side chapels.
The style is notable: rapid conception, a quick and sure line a mobility

in the figures exceptional for the
time.
We reproduce here a detail of the
sermon to the birds, full of naïveté
and grace. The trees, the leaves, the
meadow, are real and poetic at the
same time: the colour is exception-
ally modern.

wer Church: the Sermon to the Birds (Master of San Francesco).
ges 24-25: Lower Church: Interior.

THE FOUR VAULTS OR THE VAULTS OF PARADISE

Tradition, and some critics, attribute the frescoes of the vaults to Giotto himself, partly on the basis that the overhe' vault of the main altar, intended to give glory to St. Francis and his Rule, could not *not* be entrusted to the most famo' painter of his time. Others, on account of certain stylistic differences in the Master, have attributed them to Giottesco under Sienese influence, to whom, for want of better identification, they have given the name of «Master the Vaults».

Be that as it may, we must recognize that these are frescoes of high artistic value. The allegories, symbolizing Franc' can virtues, are: Chastity (a young girl in prayer inside a crenellated tower); Poverty (the mystic marriage of St. Fran' to the Lady Poverty); Obedience (the imposition of the yoke of obedience); the Triumph of St. Francis (the Sa' seated upon a throne upheld by chorusing angels).

Lower Church: The four famous vaults of the Sanctuary.

ilica of St. Francis: Tomb with the sarcophagus containing the remains of the Saint.

YPT

f way down the nave two little staircases allow us to descend to the crypt where the mortal remains of St. Francis kept. After the burial, in 1230, the stone sarcophagus containing the body of St. Francis was placed under the main r of the Lower Church.

arrow passage led to a small funerary cell; in that year, at the order of Pope Eugenius IV, this passageway was ed in, so as not to permit the body to be stolen and transported to some other place. It was a wise decision, for, ng the hostilities between communes and Signorie, it was the custom to steal even the bodies of saints from a quered town.

818 the passage was reopened, and a solemn and scientific canonical recognition was made, which, on the 5th of tember, 1820, proclaimed the identity of the body to be that of St. Francis.

und the tomb was built a crypt, in neo-Classic style, later demolished because it contrasted with the Romanesque e of the Lower Church.

as then rebuilt as it is at present, according to designs by the architect Ugo Tarchi (1925-32). This severe and dorned crypt is deeply moving, and invites us to recollection and to prayer. Four niches, dug into the stone walls he crypt, and protected by wrought-iron screens, contain the tombs of four disciples of the Saint: Leo, Ruffino, elo Tancredi and Masseo.

THE RIGHT ARM OF THE TRANSEPT

Cimabue: *The Madonna enthroned with the Child and surrounded by four angels and St. Francis.*

This is among the most celebrated works of Giotto's Master, happily saved, by reason of the reverent respect on the part of the painter commissioned to refresco the vaults. The sweetness of the Madonna's features, and of the angels', accords admirably with the solemnity of the group, to the left of which, standing alone, is painted the figure of St. Francis. The correspondence, somatic and expressive, of this figure (especially since the recent restoration which removed some ugly and arbitrary overpainting) with the physical and psychic characteristics of the Saint, according to the description in the biographer who actually knew him (Fra Tommaso da Celano), seems to convalidate the traditional belief that this was a true portrait of St. Francis. Even though one cannot speak of a portrait, in the usual sense of the term, made by a XIVth century painter, we do not regard it as reckless to accept the tradition on another level. We reprint here, for the information of the reader, the relevant passage from Fra Tommaso, *Vita* (first), Chap. XXIX, pg. 83).
«Most eloquent, merry of face and of benign aspect, neither languid nor haughty. He was of middle stature, rather on the small side; his head was round and well-shaped, his face a bit long

Lower Church. The Madonna Enthroned among Angels and St. Francis (Cimabue, about 1280).

...d prominent; his forehead was small and flat, his black eyes of a good size, with straight lashes; a straight, thin nose, ...rs jutting outward somewhat, but small; flat temples, a subtle tongue, warm and sharp, a sweet and vibrant voice, ...ar and sonorous. His teeth were white and regular, his lips small and thin, his beard black and shaven; a thin neck, ...aight shoulders, short arms, slim hands with long fingers and nails. Thin, roughly dressed ...».

GIOTTO

The great arch of the right transept, divided into two parts, was painted by a Giottesco, who worked, for the grea part of the decoration, from cartoons by the Master. The scenes refer to the infancy of Christ, to the Crucifixion, to miracles of St. Francis. We would draw the attention of the visitor to: the Nativity, the Flight into Egypt, the Cruci ion. In the fresco of the miracle of a child fallen and saved by St. Francis, to the left of the small stairway leading to Upper Church, tradition holds that the kneeling figure in the foreground represents Dante Alighieri, and the figure foot at the shoulder of the poet, Giotto himself.

Lower Church: Nativity (Giotto).

~~SI~~MONE Martini

~~Th~~ere can be no question, on the authority of Vasari himself, of the attribution to Simone Martini of the five figures of ~~sain~~ts, on the lower wall near the arch (on the right) of the entrance to the Chapel of San Nicolò.
~~Fro~~m left to right: St. Francis, St. Louis of France, St. Elizabeth, St. Clare, St. Eleazar. In the frescoes are found all the ~~cha~~racteristics of the Sienese painters: quiet sweetness, evocative force, luminous colour, aristocratic bearing in the ~~figu~~res, almond eyes.

~~Low~~er Church: The Flight into Egypt (Giotto).

Lower Church: St. Francis (Simone Martini).

wer Church: St. Clare (Simone Martini).

CHAPEL OF THE MAGDALENE

From the right transept, through a side door, one enters the Chapel of the Magdalene.
The frescoes, restored recently to their early splendour, are ascribed to Giotto and his students. Of certain attribution to the Master, both in conception and execution, is the figure of the Magdalene, shown with Bishop Pontorno, commissioner of the Chapel, at her feet.
Particularly in evidence, on the upper righthand wall, is the «*Noli me tangere*» scene, made the more dramatic by the outstretched eagerness of the hands of the Magdalene in her desire to touch the garments of the risen Christ.

*Lower Church
Chapel of the
Magdalene -
Resurrection
Lazarus
(Giotto).*

Chapel of the Magdalene: The Bishop of Assisi, Tebaldo Pontano, the comissioner of the Chapel, at the feet of the Magdalene (Giotto).

Chapel of the Magdalene: Noli me tangere (Giotto).

EFT ARM OF THE TRANSEPT

[I]we retrace our steps and recross the sanctuary, we reach the left transept.

[Th]is transept, frescoed by the Sienese Pietro Lorenzetti, arouses at first glance an intense, almost disturbing, sense of [w]onder, both for its liveliness and the luminosity of his colour. His palette is as rich and varied as that of Duccio, from [w]hich it seems drawn.

[Th]e paintings executed around 1320 represent scenes from the Passion of Christ. The scenes are in two sectors: [be]fore and after the death of Christ. In the frescoes representing the episodes «before the death of Christ» some critics [di]scern the hand of Ambrogio, the brother of Pietro. The frescoes that chiefly claim our attention are: the Crucifixion [u]nfortunately mutilated in 1607, when a baroque altar was set up), a work of great spaciousness and exceptional nar[ra]tive effectiveness; under the Cross there is a «sacred conversation» between the personages, in attitudes of contain[ed] and reflective sorrow; it is particularly interesting to examine the personages individually, both for their expres[si]ons and the costumes they wear.

[Le]ft-hand page: *Lower Church: The left transept, frescoed by Pietro Lorenzetti.*
[Be]low: *Lower Church: The great Crucifixion, by Pietro Lorenzetti.*

Lower Church: The Triumphal Entry of Jesus into Jerusalem (Pietro Lorenzetti).

...wer Church: The Deposition from the Cross by Pietro Lorenzetti. This fresco is to be seen on the lower wall, to the left ...the arch leading into the Orsini Chapel: in a solemn and composed rhythm the personages express their pain with ...iching drama.

MADONNA OF THE SUNSET

So-called because at the sunset hour the image is illuminated by the rays of the sun filtering through a window th[at] faces it. It is the masterpiece of Lorenzetti, for the grace and sweetness of the figure, for its expressive effectivene[ss] for the luminosity and transparency of the colours. The Madonna, with the Child in her arms, has at her right St. Fra[n]cis, and at her left, St. John the Evangelist. The face of the Madonna, suffused with tenderness, is turned toward h[er] Son in an attitude suggesting both that she is answering and questioning: the Mother seems to respond by turni[ng] toward St. Francis the thumb of her right hand. It is a sacred conversation that lends itself to many interpretations.

Lower Church: the Madonna of the Sunset by Pietro Lorenzetti.

UPPER CHURCH

One ascends to the Upper Church by means of one of the stairways placed in the end wall of the transept.
By this means one reaches the next level, containing the Cloister of Sixtus IV, placed at the shoulder of an imposi apse in rose and white stone of Subasio. Following the stairs one finds oneself in the arm of the transept of the Up Church. The Church is in Gothic style, a single nave divided into four sections.
One is struck immediately by the contrast between the luminosity of this Church and the mystical half-light of t lower one.
The play of light and colour, the architectural movement created by the slender Gothic columns and airy ribbing, t large polychromed windows of glass, call forth our joyous admiration.
The Church is entirely frescoed, with a harmonious sequence of frescoes and decorations.
During the XIII and XIV centuries there laboured here the greatest artists of the time: Cimabue, Giotto, Piet Cavallini, Jacopo Turriti, Filippo Rusuti.

Basilica of St. Francis: Cloister of Sixtus IV (XV C.) and apse.
Basilica of St. Francis: The Arcade (XIII C.); in the background the Umbrian plain, traversed by the winding Tescio

THE LEFT ARM OF THE TRANSEPT

The left arm of the transept was painted by Cimabue, who worked in Assisi, at considerable intervals of time, f
1278 to 1285.
The frescoes have suffered grave deterioration, in the darkening of the light parts, due to the chemical alteratio
white lead because of dampness. The great Crucifixion, notwithstanding the diminution, is the most important w
of the Master, a testimony of the moment of his fullest artistic maturity. It is a highly dramatic composition, in
«frightening» Cimabuesque manner.
Also by Cimabue are the four frescoes of the vault of the transept: the cities represented in the vaults anticipate
plastic strength of his pupil, Giotto.

Upper Church: Crucifixion (Cimabue).

Upper Church: The Choir.

Upper Church: Two stalls of the Choir, in inlaid wood.

Following pages: The splendid interior of the Upper Church.

e Frescoes of Giotto. - The fame of the Upper Church is closely linked to the work of Giotto, d vice-versa: the two are inseparable.

e frescoes represent the first two artistic phases of Giotto; the third, that of his maturity, was ieved at Padua, in the Scrovegni Chapel.

e first stay of Giotto in Assisi is set at around 1282, when he was about twenty-five years of age. him were entrusted the third and fourth upper abutments (beginning at the altar). In the third itment, the first to be frescoed, Giotto already expresses a new conception of plasticity and a ee-dimensional sense of space.

rticularly celebrated, and astonishing to his contemporaries, is the hand of the Lord, projecting though to touch the space outside the frame surrounding Him. In the fourth abutment, Giotto enuates the strength of the composition and turns his attention to the poetry of the landscape. e young Giotto is here in Assisi, sincere, full of vigor and with multiple interests.

otto, after rendering the scene of Isaac, painted the vault of the Doctors (the first to be seen m the doorway), and here we find an attempt to draw the buildings in perspective. It was an eresting intuition, even though he failed: two centuries had to pass before the laws governing rspective were to be discovered.

otto was the real inventor of pictorial art; he discovered the tridimensionality of space, investi- ed the plasticity and mass of the figure, gave light and shadow and subtlety to his colours, and roduced landscape as an element of the composition.

Left-hand page:
Upper Church:
Stained glass of
the rigth
transept-Scenes
from the Old
Testament -
Episodes from
the Life of Jesus.

Below:
Upper Church:
Isaac Repulses
Esau (Giotto,
about 1292).

His second stay has been set in the period between 1297 and 1299, before the Jubilee year which saw him called to Rome by Pope Boniface VIII. He was entrusted with the frescoing of the lower part of the nave, the most important part, as a result of the praise heaped upon him for his work of fifteen years before, and of his high fame both in Florence and in Rome. In twenty-eight scenes, each measuring 3,67 meters in height, and almost the same in width, is told the story of St. Francis, according to the «Great Legend» of St. Bonaventure (1221-1274). These were composed on the basis of the first biographer, Tommaso da Celano, and drawn from the oral tradition already very much alive among the people of Assisi, and from the accounts of his brothers in religion who had known the Saint personally.

Upper Church: The Vault with the Doctors of the Church by Giotto, damaged by the earthquake of 26th. September 1997.

VAULTING-CELL WITH ST. JEROME: A DETAIL OF THE VAULT WITH THE DOCTORS OF THE CHURCH BY GIOTTO, WHICH COLLAPSED DURING THE EARTHQUAKE OF 26TH. SEPTEMBER 1997

THE GIOTTESQUE SEQUENCE OF THE LIFE OF ST. FRANCIS

The sequence of the frescoes begins on the wall, at the height of the main altar.
We shall make a very short comment on panel, where it is necessary, explaining the gnificance of the scene in the life of the Sair

1) THE YOUNG FRANCIS IS HONOURED BY THE SIMPLE OF THE TOWN

In the chronology of the execution of the this was one of the last frescoes to be exec at a time when Giotto had already been call Rome by Pope Boniface VIII. The design Giotto, but the execution that of one o students, though one of considerable excell

Upper Church: the Creator, sinopite (Rc Master, about 1290).

to whom, for lack of better identification, been given the name, «Master of Saint Cec from the icon of that saint in the Uffizi Galler Florence.

This icon bears a perfect graphic likeness to of the fresco: small head, small and penetra eyes. In the background can be seen the Ten of Minerva, with five columns rather than six, the Public Square of the town. The scene trace episode of which San Bonaventura speaks in first chapter of the Great Legend:

«... a man of Assisi, very simple-minded, spr out his cloak and his clothing at the feet of Fra and declared him worthy of veneration. declared that he was destined by Heaven to g things, and to be honoured in all the world».

2) THE SAINT GIVES HIS CLOAK TO A POOR KNIGHT

Here is a new kind of drawing; the expression Francis's face is one of sweetness, astonished wondering that of the poor horseman; the ho placidly goes on cropping grass. The use landscape in the composition should be noted, this was a new step for Giotto. The space bounded by a small rocky city on the left, an town and bell tower on the right.

«Restored to health, elegantly dressed, as always, day he left his house. On the road he met a knigh noble aspect, but poor and badly dressed, as u Francis did not hesitate an instant. He took off rich mantle and clothing and with these covered miserable man». (St. Bonaventure, Ibid, I, pg. 2).

3) THE DREAM OF ARMS

«The following night, after the above gift, Fra had a dream from God. He seemed to see a splen and beautiful palace containing within it me weapons, all signed with crosses... Francis as the meaning of all these arms, and a voice fr Heaven answered: "You and your followers"».

Francis didn't understand the meaning of reply from God, who wished him to form Order of ardent defenders of the faith; inste Francis thought mistakenly of some earthly glo and left to join, in Puglia, the soldier of fortu Gualtiero di Brienne.

When he reached Spoleto, however, the sa voice admonished him to return to Assisi.

) St. Francis prays before the crucifix of San Damiano

Having returned from Spoleto to Assisi, one day ~~h~~e went out into the country to meditate, and ~~fo~~und himself near the little Church of San Dami-~~a~~no, which was threatened by the ruin of age. ~~In~~spired by God, he entered the Church and, at the ~~fe~~et of the Crucifix, praying with great fervor, he ~~fe~~lt his soul fill with joy. Then he raised up his tear-~~fu~~l eyes, and he heard in his ear a mysterious ~~vo~~ice. That voice came down from the lips of the ~~cr~~ucified Christ, and was addressed to himself. ~~Th~~ree times it repeated. "Francis, restore my house ~~th~~at, as you see, is falling into ruin"».

~~Th~~e angular perspective of the Church and the ~~di~~sposition of the masses in its interior testify to ~~th~~e study Giotto gave to the understanding of ~~sp~~aces.

) St. Francis returns his clothing to his father

~~Fr~~ancis was brought to judgment before the ~~B~~ishop of Assisi, by his father.

~~...~~until such time as he should renounce his patri-~~m~~ony and return to his father everything that he ~~sti~~ll owned... he did not wait for a sentence; he did ~~n~~ot defend himself. In a flash, he undressed ~~hi~~mself and handed back his clothing to his ~~fa~~ther... to whom he said: "Until now I have called ~~yo~~u, on this earth, father; henceforth I can say, in ~~al~~l truth: "Our Father, who art in Heaven, in ~~w~~hom I have reposed all my goods and all my ~~co~~nfidence". At this unexpected gesture by the ~~m~~an of God, the Bishop, a good and pious man, ~~sp~~rang to his feet and ran in tears to embrace ~~Fr~~ancis, and to wrap him in his own mantle».

~~Th~~is one of the most dramatic scenes: the gesture ~~of~~ Francis, so unexpected, sets in motion both the ~~B~~ishop and Pietro di Bernardone. Giotto caught ~~th~~e moment following the swift action: the thrust ~~of~~ Francis' arms, raised and with joined hands, to ~~h~~eaven; the angry movement of the father, yellow ~~in~~ the face with rage (the first time that a ~~ps~~ychological value is given to a particular co-~~lo~~ur); the rocklike body of the Bishop, witnesses ~~to~~ an event that was to be so resounding; the ~~fa~~ces, mute and incredulous, of the bystanders. ~~E~~ven the two buildings seem to participate in the ~~d~~rama, jutting forward as they do, in a singular ~~p~~erspective.

6) Innocent III sees in a dream the Saint sustaining the fallin Lateran

After the restitution of his clothing to his father, Franc dressed in the dun-coloured smock of the Umbrian pe ant, with a hood on his head and a cord tied about waist, began his evangelizing sermons in his nati town. All his discourses opened with the greeting Pax Bonum (Peace and Goodness): that sweet salutati would constitute the teaching of the Franciscan mov ment. In the hearts of the citizens, who had forme despised him and driven him away, regarding him a madman, that salutation and his preachings began take hold. Among the first who asked to follow h were the Assisan nobleman, Bernardo di Quintaval then Pietro Cattani, the legal counsellor of the Chapt Egidio, Sabatino, Morico, Giovanni da Campello.

When his followers reached the number of eleven, Fra cis decided that he should request authorization from t Pope to charter a Rule of life for his brothers. In t month of May of 1209, he left with them from Rivotor where he had founded his first tiny convent, called Tug rio, and went to Rome. Innocent III orally, approved, t Rule, after some initial doubts arising from what regarded as its excessive rigour.

The Curia, in fact, wished to act with great pruden since some preceding religious movements, that of t Waldensians, for example, had given rise to grave he sies. The doubts were resolved by a vision of the Po *«.. . he saw in a dream the Lateran Basilica threaten with ruin, and a poor man, small and unimpressive, w upheld it on his shoulders. "It is surely this one", said t Pope, "who will bolster up the Church, and sustain h with his works and doctrine"».* (Ibid. II, 10).

Two masses and two actions: one, static, draws attenti to the tranquil dream of the Pontiff, in the profou silence of the cubicle; the other, dynamic, exalts t action of Francis.

7) Innocent III approves the rule of the Friars Minor

Among the frescoes of Giotto, this is one of the m important.

The sense of space is given an admirable rhythm consoles and arches: the depth of the scene, occupied two facing groups of differing volumes, would appear set In evidence the papal majesty and the grateful hum ity of Francis.

8) The vision of the fiery chariot

«In the Tugurio of Rivotorto, Francis being absent, t friars in prayer, toward midnight, see enter the door a circle the room three times a splendid fiery chari crowned by a globe like the sun, that changed night in day». (Ibid. IV, 4).

THE VISION OF THE HEAVENLY CHAIRS

Pacifico saw St. Francis carried away into ecstasy during [pray]er. Then *«.. . he saw opened to his eyes Heaven, and [am]ong the innumerable thrones, one that was particularly [noti]ceable. It was the most beautiful, all adorned with pre[ciou]s stones, and shining with light. A voice told him: "This [thro]ne belonged to one of the rebel angels, and now it is re[serv]ed to humble Francis"».* (Ibid. VI, 6).

[10]) THE EXPULSION OF THE DEMONS FROM AREZZO

[It c]ame about that Francis, the man of God, went to Arezzo, [whe]n that city, torn with internal struggles, was approaching [cert]ain disaster. From the outskirts, where he had taken lodg[ing] Francis saw a number of demons jumping joyfully about [in th]e air. It was these who were prompting the citizens to their [event]ual destruction. To disperse them Francis sent Fra Silve[ster]. "Go", he said, "to the gate of the city and command them [in t]he name of the Almighty, and in obedience, to leave the [plac]e at once, and go far away Peace at once came to the [city,] and the citizens in all courtesy set about restoring civil [righ]ts to all».* (Ibid. VI, 9). The mediaeval city of Arezzo, belted [with c]renellated walls, with its sterometric panorama of houses, [tow]ers and Churches, constituted an example of the new [giot]tesque course of interpretation of space and of solids.

11) St. Francis before the Sultan

Francis, who had always desired martyrdom, went to Egypt, in the year 1219, to preach the Gospel. He was arrested and brought before the Sultan Melek-el-Kamel, and with great courage affirmed that he had come to Egypt to proclaim the Gospel, and to lead his people away from the teachings of Mohammed. He requested, as proof of the truth of his beliefs, an ordeal by fire… «*I order you to build the largest possible fire. Then I will walk into the flames with all my priests; that way at least I can convince you which law and which faith is most true, most holy and most worthy to be followed*». (Ibid. IX,)

12) The ecstasy of St. Francis

«*Sometimes he was seen in prayer, at night, with his arms outspread to form a cross, and raised from the ground, surrounded by a small, shining cloud…*» (Ibid. X, 4).
This panel is evidently the work of one of Giotto's helpers, to judge by its poor force of expression.

13) St. Francis makes the first Christmas Crib scene at Greccio

On the Christmas of 1223 «*Three years before his death, Francis wished to represent, in a living tableau, at Greccio, and with the greatest solemnity, the Nativity of the Christ Child... He therefore prepared a humble straw-filled manger, and placed there an ox and an ass.*» (Ibid X, 7).

This holy way of recalling the crib of the first Christmas entered, from that time on, into the regular, and among the most beloved, customs of the Christian world.

The spatial effect, set in relief by the high-placed cross and by the lectern, the mobile figure tenderly embracing the Child, are the most notable parts of the painting. In other parts, the diversity of the workmanship suggests the almost certain intervention of various helpers.

Pag. 60

14) The miracle of the spring

Another time, Francis wished to go to a certain ermitage, the more freely to devote himself to contemplation. But he was weak, and so was forced to hire a poor man's donkey for the ride. On that hot summer day, and because of the long, steep mountainous path, the owner of the donkey, who was following on foot, felt faint. Finally, he could go no farther, and began to wail loudly: *"I am dying of thirst. If I don't have water soon, I shall die".* Francis sprang to the ground at once and, falling to his knees, with his hands and his eyes raised to Heaven, he prayed until he knew that he had been heard by God. *"Hurry, he said to the poor man, 'run to that rock. There you will find living water that at this very moment, out of His goodness, Christ has made to flow for you' "»* Ibid. VII, 12).

The transposition of the tale of St. Bonaventure to the frescoed panel is perfect. The pictorial comment is admirable. The hard rough rocks, divided by a corner of sky, accompany, with their symmetrical thrust, the prayer of the saint. The impetus of the thirsty man as he throws himself down to the stream to satisfy the thirst he has suffered so long, is reminiscent, even in its sculptural force, of the thirsty figures by Arnolfo on the fonte Maggiore in Perugia. The two plump friars, behind a tired and apathetic donkey, constitute an earthly counterweight to the miraculous event.

Pag. 61

15) The sermon to the birds

Near Bevagna the Saint chanced upon a flock of birds, of various kinds, perched on the trees and feeding in the meadow. At once he was surrounded by them, as though they had some reason for greeting him kindly... standing among them, he exhorted them with fervor to be quiet a little and to listen to the word of God: My little brothers, you should greatly praise the Lord. He has covered you with feathers, and has given you wings for flying; he has given the air to you, and he has prepared food for you without labour on your part». While he was speaking to them in this way, the birds, with a marvelous demonstration of love, stretched out their necks, and spread their wings, opened their beaks and watched him attentively... then he made the sign of the Cross and blessed them all. Joyously the birds flew into the air, all together, singing» (Ibid. XII, 3).

This is the most celebrated painting of the cycle. Giotto, so concrete and realistic, not at all sentimental, in picturing the sermon to the birds was unexpectedly moved, and out of this feeling issued a highly lyrical work of art.

16) THE DEATH OF THE KNIGHT OF CELANO

«… he went to pray at Celano, where he was invited to dine with a devout knight. Francis accepted and, in an action truly singular in an ordinary mortal, invited the knight to confess himself, in preparation for death.
Finally they were seated at table, and the others had begun to eat, when the host, just as Francis had foretold, fell dead suddenly» (Ibid. XI, 4).

The highly dramatic scene is accentuated by the architectural effect of the small loggia projecting over the table. To be noted are the table, laid out as for a banquet, and the table linens embroidered In the "Assisi stitch", still employed by the craftswomen of the town.

17) THE SERMON BEFORE POPE HONORIUS III

«Once, urged by Signor Ostiense, the Saint learned by memory a discourse very artfully prepared, to be spoken before the Pope and the Cardinals. But when he found himself in the midst of them, he forgot the speech, and remained as though mute. After humbly confessing his lapse of memory, he besought the Holy Spirit, Whereupon he became a stream of apostolic eloquence, and the words fell from his lips so effectively that all his highly placed hearers were greatly moved» (Ibid. XII, 7).

Another fresco entirely painted by the artist is this one. The Pope is seated on a throne, in a composed and throughtful attitude; he has an exceptional importance of mass in a space created by the central perspective of the arches of the vault.

18) THE APPEARANCE AT THE CHAPTER-MEETING AT ARLES

«Francis never attended the meetings of the Provincial Chapters… but occasionally, he would appear, even visibly, by a marvelous work of God, and so it was that he came to the Chapter-Meeting of Arles, where the Blessed Anthony of Padua was speaking to the friars» (Ibid. IV, 10).

This work must be attributed to a mediocre helper.

19) ST. FRANCIS RECEIVES THE STIGMATA ON MOUNT AVERNA

On the 14th of September of 1224… while Francis was praying on the side of Mount Averna, he saw descending from the sky a Seraphim with six burning and brilliant wings, The flight was very swift… and he saw amid the wings the figure of a man with his hands and his feet stretched and nailed upon a cross. Two wings were raised over his head, two were opened for flight, and two covered his body. The Saint marvelled at this sight, and he was seized by a joy mingled with pain… When the

on disappeared, there were left in the flesh of the *t, In his hands and feet, the signs of the nails that he* *seen in the figure of the crucified Man* (Ibid. XIII, 3).

y the figure of the Saint is held to be by the artist self; there is to be noted, however, a handling of e that accords well with the event.

) THE DEATH OF ST. FRANCIS

re being finally completed in him all the divine plans, *most holy soul escaped the holy body and was* *med Into the glory of Heaven, and the body lay as in* *ft sleep. One of the friars and disciples saw that soul* *nd, like a brilliant star upon a white cloud, hasten-* *o Heaven»* (Ibid. XIV, 6).

ne lower part of the composition, there is to be noted gorous plasticity in the figures: the middle part, over- vded, denotes the hands of the helpers.

21) IN THE HOUR OF HIS PASSING

«… also the Superior of the Friars of Terr[a di]
Lavoro, Augustine by name, a man of g[reat]
holiness, himself at the point of death, [and]
for some time unable to speak, was he[ard]
suddenly to exclaim: "Wait for me, O [the]
father, wait for me; look, I'm coming [to]
you". He appeared also on the same nig[ht to]
the Bishop of Assisi, then on a pilgrima[ge to]
Gargano» (Ibid. XIV, 6).

The two episodes are shown in the s[ame]
panel, which is of mediocre execution.

22) THE CONFIRMATION OF THE STIGMATA

«A certain knight, by name Girolam[o, a]
literary man and very famous, who [had]
doubted, incredulous as Thomas had b[een,]
with great fervor and courage, in fro[nt of]
everyone, friars and laymen, made sur[e of]
the Stigmata on the hands, and touche[d the]
feet and the side of the Saint, to dispel [every]
shadow of doubt, his own or anyone el[se's»]
(ibid. XV, 1).

23) THE BODY OF ST. FRANCIS CARRIED T[O] ASSISI ON THE MORNIN[G] AFTER HIS DEATH

«Passing by the little Church of San Da[mi]
ano, where the noblewoman Clare, [now]
glorious in Heaven, enclosed herself [with]
her virgins, the cortege stopped a whil[e so]
that his spiritual daughters could see [and]
kiss the holy body of their father».
(Ibid. XV, 5).

The design is by Giotto; this can be re[cog]
nized from the expressive force of [the]
central group and the architectural line[s of]
the Church.

24) THE CANONIZATION OF THE SAINT

«Pope Gregory IX came personally to Assisi, and o Sunday, the 16th of July, 1228, with the greatest soler nity, wrote the blessed father into the Calendar of Sain (Ibid. XV, 8).*

This panel, and the successive ones, are the work Giotto's pupils, as the master had been called to Rome Boniface VIII for the Jubilee celebrations.

25) THE APPARITION TO GREGORY IX

«Pope Gregory IX... was beset by a doubt regarding t. wound in the side. One night there appeared to him t. Blessed Francis, frowning. He banished the doubt, ra ing his right arm and displaying the wound».
(Ibid. Mir. I, 2).

26) THE SAINT HEALS A WOUNDED MA

«A certain Giovanni di Lerida of Catalogna, grave wounded and dying, invokes the Saint. Saint Franc appears to him...» he draws near, removes the dressin and applies an ointment to the wounds.
At the soothing touch of those hands the flesh regains soundness and the wounds are smoothly scarred (Ib. Mir. I, 5).

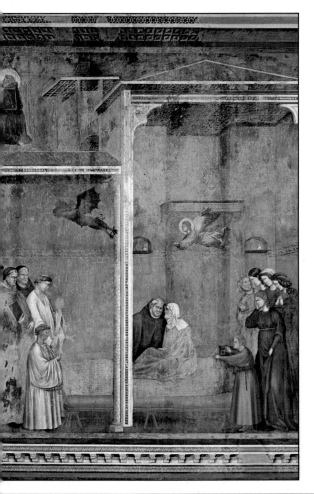

7) THE CONFESSION OF A DEAD WOMAN RESTORED TO LIFE

*under the eyes of everyone, the dead woman sat up in
d and spoke to a priest who was present: Come closer,
ther, and hear a sin of mine that I never confessed in
v lifetime. I would have had to suffer a harsh penalty,
t St. Francis, as a reward for my devotion, gained me
· grace to awaken in order to confess my sin and reach
aven the sooner."* (Ibid Mir. II, 1).

28) THE LIBERATION OF THE PENITENT HERETIC

«*All the logs broke into pieces, the doors opened without
being touched and the way out was cleared*».
(Ibid, Mir. V, 5).
The last two panels are attributed to the Master of St.
Cecilia.

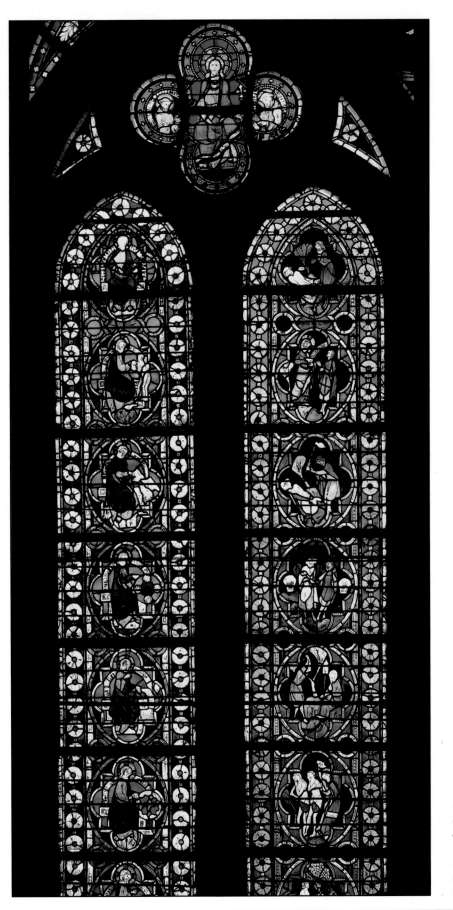

Upper Church: Stained glass of left transept - Scenes from Gen and Female Saints.

Upper Church: Stained glass of nave (first to the right) - Scenes fr the Life of St. Francis (detail).

Upper Church: Stained glass of the nave (first to the right) - Scenes from the Life of St. Francis, detail of the Saint Preaching to the Birds.

Upper Church: The rose window of the façade seen from the inside of the church.

ÇADE OF THE UPPER CHURCH

ning out of the Upper Church, we find before us a great field, gently sloping upward.
façade, of a warm golden colour, is very simple in its architectural structure.
he base is a double door; above, at the second level, is a splendid rose-window, of Cosmatesque work, with the
ns of the four Evangelists at the sides; in the pediment is a round window, smaller in size; on the left a small 18th
tury loggia with a dome, which, though of a completely different style, seems to amalgamate with the whole.
inviting to pause a moment at the summit of the double marble staircase that joins the Piazza San Francesco with
field in front of the Upper Church, in order to have a look at the complex of the Basilica beside us, with a bird's-
view of the Umbrian plain below, from which emerges the high cupola of the Basilica of Santa Maria degli Angeli.

INSIDE THE CITY

Before passing on to the centre
the city, it would be as well to ta
a look at the plan of Assisi (encl
ed with this book) to get a bet
sense of orientation.

It is a mediaeval city, surrounded
a city wall, the perimeter of which
some 5 kilometers. There are ei
city gates with high towers a
battlements from which they w
formerly defended. The pres
perimeter shows the expansion
the city in the period of its great
splendor, which was, as we ha
noted, rudely interrupted after t
sacking by Piccinino in 1492. In t
time of St. Francis the extent of c
wall was much smaller: of the
walls there are only a few remai
including the gates we find insi
the city. The street plan is authen
cally mediaeval: the two princi
longitudinal streets intersect at t
center of the city, in the Piazza c
Comune, and from these exter
transversely, steep and narr
streets, often with steps, that le
directly to the walls. The city w
divided into six sectors, and to ea
sector was entrusted a stretch of w
to be defended. The function of t
small streets, direct and perpendic
lar, was to make it possible
defenders to reach the wall rapid
in case of a sudden assault.

We suggest that the tourist go ir
the ancient parts of the city, a
pause and visit the little streets: it
to immerse oneself in an authen
mediaeval atmosphere. The c
houses, usually constructed in dre
ed Subasio stone, and set in horizo
tal rows, have very beautiful doo
with round or pointed arches, a
finely chiselled borders. The wi
dows, with lower arches, are of t
same material. The walls, decorat
with cornices, water holders a
brackets, often darkened by the fi
set during sackings and factior
quarrels. There are no symmetric
structures, since the houses we
often altered or rebuilt in the cour
of the centuries: the numerous doc
and windows bricked up, and t
buttressing, bear witness to this. T
pottery roof tiles and gutte
(samples of which we have se

...ulptured in stone at the base of the ...vic Tower) project over the streets, ...ld up by wooden supports.

...ear the principal door, at the height ...about a meter from the ground ...oor, there is a smaller door, in the ...me style (nowadays usually ...icked up), called the «door of the ...ead», since, according to local ...stom, the body of the dead in-...bitant was carried out for burial ...rough this narrow little elevated ...oor. This symbolized that the soul ...the former inhabitant, who before ...ath had entered by the principal ...oor, remained in the house near the ...mily, almost like a household god ...the Romans. Another interpreta-...on, less poetic but more logical, ...olds rather that this was an ...trance intended for defense: it was ...pproached by means of a mobile ...dder of sticks, which was pulled ...before bolting the doors with ...oss-bars and timbers.

...umerous arches link houses that ...ce each other. All these structures, ...varied and strange, create an ...ocative and poetic atmosphere. ...e mediaeval character of the cons-...ctions, austere and plain, is sweet-...ed by flowers and ornamental ...ants: on every window, every ...lcony or little loggia, grows a ...ofusion of geraniums, carnations, ...nging bellflowers, which the ...omen of Assisi, custodians of a ...dition of gentleness, cultivate with ...re and love.

ROM THE BASILICA OF ...T. FRANCIS TO THE ...IAZZA DEL COMUNE

...ne ascends to the Piazza del ...omune along the Via San ...ancesco.
...n the sides of the street, once ...lled the Via Superba (Proud), as ...ell as the XVIII century houses of ...e nobles, now become schools, ...e see on the left the house of the ...omancini Masters of the XIV ...entury, the town Library, rich in ...recious manuscripts and *incuna-* ...*oli;* on the right, the Pilgrim's ...ratory of the Mezastris, and the XIV ...entury colonnade of Mount ...umentario.

ROMAN FORUM

On the left, before reaching the Piazza del Comune, in the surviving crypt of the Church of San Nicolò, has been s
up the Roman Museum, where are kept the findings from the times of the Etruscans and the Romans: funerary urn
carved stones, sarcophagae, sepulchral pillars, altars, clay objects, etc. Through a subterranean passage one pass
to the ancient Forum, which testifies to the splendor of the Roman township. There is an interesting mural paintin
by means of which, and on the basis of remaining architectural elements, it can be reconstructed.

Head of Jove.
The Crypt of S. Nicolò, now the Roman Museum.

Stone to the Legionnaire Cottiedius Attianus, who died
twenty years of age and Etruscan Funerary Urn.

THE TEMPLE OF MINERVA

...as constructed in the first century A. D., and dedicated to the goddess Minerva by the brothers Tiro and Cesio Prisco. ...is an elegant temple, in the Corinthian style, with six high columns sustaining the entablature and the pediment. ...he steps leading to the vestibule, fitted into the plinths of the columns are an unusual feature. ...he capitals are very beautiful, and well-preserved. The temple is now consecrated as a Christian Church (Santa Maria ...opra Minerva). The baroque ornamentations of the interior are a real disappointment.

PIAZZA DEL COMUNE

Once arrived in the Piazza, our gaze is drawn to the Palazzo del Capitano del Popolo (Palace of the People's Captain), with its high Civic Tower and the Temple of Minerva. It is a happy combination, though representing two very different styles and periods.

On the other side of the Piazza is the Palazzo dei Priori (Palace of the Priors), comprising a number of buildings, of XIV century construction.

CHIESA NUOVA AND ORATORY OF S. FRANCESCO PICCOLINO

Both of these are found behind Palazzo dei Priori, on the left. pretty little Church, of baroque sty in the form of a Greek Cross, built through the generosity of Ph III of Spain in the XVII century, the ruins of the paternal house of Francis.

Inside is shown «the prison», a d and narrow cell where, according tradition, Pietro di Bernardone prisoned Francis after the you man had sold some bolts of preci materials in order to restore, with proceeds, the little Church of Damiano. The little convent of Friars Minor, adjacent to the Chur contains the shop, the bedroom the Saint, and a mediaeval lane.

S. FRANCESCO PICCOLIN

A stable, also belonging to Pietro Bernardone, where, according to long and pious tradition, St. Fran was born to Madonna Pica. Unde fine half-pointed arch, on the sto border, in the Gothic lett employed at the end of the X

Bottom: *S. Francesco Piccolino: The stall in which, according to tradition, St. Francis was born. The three entranceways to the paternal house of St.Francis.*

ntury, one reads, in Latin: «In this Oratory, once the stall of an ox and an ass, was born Francis, a light to the world».
e Oratory is served by the Conventual Friars Minor. From the Piazza anyone who has the time is advised to make a
ort digression from the principal itinerary. By way of the Via San Paolo, descending some steps on the left, we
ach the small Church of S. Stefano. The inside, which contains a small nave, with semicircular apse, unadorned,
th slit-windows, is calm and evocative. Tradition has it that one of the bells of the little belltower, blowing in the
nd, tolled the death of St. Francis.

turning to the Piazza del Comune, one ascends the narrow Via S. Rufino, so characteristic of the town, to the
urch of San Rufino.

e small Church of S. Stefano (XII c.).

Cathedral of St. Ruphinus

At the base of a rectangular Piazza, flanked by two modest buildings, adorned in stonework, rises the magnificent and severe façade, in Romanesque-Umbrian style, of the Cathedral of San Rufino. It provides the most beautiful stage imaginable for sacred performances, such as the recitation of the hymns of Fra Jacopone of Todi, which are normally given on August evenings on the occasion of the liturgical festivities of San Rufino, patron saint of the city.

As we learn from an engraved stone, in beautiful Gothic characters, set into the wall at the base of the nave, on the right, the construction of the Cathedral was begun in the year 1140. «Rainiero being the Prior and the architect being Giovanni di Gubbio». It is unusal to find the name of the architect mentioned: in any case, it removes all doubt concerning the attribution of the work.

The Church destined to receive the remains of the martyr Bishop St. Rufinus, who preached the Gospel in Assisi in the first half of the III century, and who was drowned in the river Chiascio by his persecutors, is, chronologically, the third Church to be dedicated to the saint, after a small chapel of the V century and the Church of Ugone of the XI century.

THE FAÇADE

The façade merits a careful examination, considering its significance and its importance in the history of art.
Vertically it is divided by pilasters into three parts, corresponding to the three naves in the interior; horizontally, it is also divided into three zones, defined by the cornices of small, typically Romanesque arches. In the lower sector, divided into three panels, three doors are opened in the façade, at the base of which are lions and griffons bearing columns. The central portal is an important sculptural masterpiece, given that it represents the beginning of a new epoch in art: the rough barbaric forms of the high mediaeval style fall before the reawakening generated by the rediscovery of the classical, in the climate of communal liberty reaffirming the personality of man.

THE CAMPANILE OR BELLTOWER

The strong belltower is entirely worthy of the façade: it is set on a robust Roman foundation, consisting of huge blocks of travertine marvelously fitted together. The perfection of this construction (visible from the inside) is such that it would seem possible to use it as a cistern. The belltower was once a part of the Church of Ugone, but it was not high then; this is deduced from examination of the ornamentation of unsquared stone.
The part above the cornice (over the clock), ornamented with cut stone, was built at the same time as the façade, and is in perfect harmony with it. There are interesting double windows in the bell-chamber, above four rows of blind arches meant to give greater élan to the architectural structure.

THE LUNETTE OF THE CENTRAL PORTAL

Christ is enthroned between the sun and moon, symbolizing Christ the King and H[igh] Priest, light in darkness.

At the right: the Madonna nurses the Child, sig[ni]fying the Church as Mother.

To the left: the Bishop, who interprets the doctr[ine] of Christ.

Some critics hold that the bas-reliefs came fr[om] the preceding Church of Ugone, because the b[ase] does not match the architrave, and because [its] rough expressive power seems to resemble tha[t of] barbaric sculpture. Others dissent, arguing t[hat] the sculpture has the stylistic and symbolic char[ac]ter of the twelfth century; and that the stone-cu[tter] followed the designs of Giovanni da Gubbio, [but] simply mistook the measurements.

Similar observations can be made as to the upri[ght] columns and the lions upholding them, differ[ing] in volume and in height, and not in per[fect] symmetry with the parts.

The two lions of the principal door are superb[ly] polished red stone, symbolizing the Christ w[ho] abolished pagan sacrifices, bloody or human ([the] lion looking to the left); and the Hebraic sacri[fice] of a scapegoat (the lion to the right).

ENTER SECTION OF FAÇADE

eries of small suspended arches, surmounted by an airy loggia with small columns whose capitals are full of asy, divide the lower section from the center one.

central rose-window, of exquisite workmanship, is surrounded by the symbols of the four Evangelists, and held» by three caryatids, symbolizing the Old Testament: on either side are two rose-windows, meant to illuminate lateral naves, before the reconstruction of the interior.

er small arches define this mass from the pediment, at the center of which was built, at the end of the XIII century, ogival arch not intended in the original design of Giovanni da Gubbio.

urch of St. Ruphinus: Detail of façade.

CHAPEL OF THE MADONNA OF TEARS

This chapel is to the left, in the Sanctuary, a
holds a Pietà in polychromed terracotta,
German workmanship of the middle of the
century. According to tradition, this stat
wept in 1494, during some cruel interneci
wars.

CHAPEL OF THE SACRAMENT

In baroque style, this chapel was built in
XVII century and designed by Giorgetti.
Large paintings by Andrea Carloni hang on
walls.

SACRISTY AND ORATORY OF SAN FRANCESCO

In the main room of the Sacristy hangs an
painting by Sermei. «Saint FrancIs blessi
Assisi». From the Sacristy one descends to t
Oratory of St. Francis, where the saint oft
remained in prayer and meditation, befc
preaching to the people of Assisi.

Church of St. Ruphinus: Pietà, in polychromed terracotta (German. XV c.).
Church of St. Ruphinus: Baptismal Font.

Church of St. Ruphinus. A "misericord" in the choir.

CAPITOLARE MUSEUM

Here is kept a tryptich by Nicolò Liberatore, called Alunno; there are other notable paintings, and an archive containing precious parchments of the X and XI centuries.

THE CRYPT OF THE CHURCH OF UGONE

In order to visit the Church of Ugone one must be accompanied by the Sacristan. The Church was constructed in the XI century, and is to be found five meters under the present level of the Cathedral. The nave, including the apse, was forty feet long by twenty feet wide. The crypt is led into by a small door of Carolingian style, with an arch and double ring, and with Dutch capitals. In the interior of the crypt, of severe Romanesque style, is to be found a sarcophagus of the Roman epoch (III century), with fine relief sculptures representing the myth of Diana and Endymion. In the apse the traces of the primitive paintings.

Church of St. Ruphinus: The little Carolingian arcade of the Church of Ugone (XI c.).
Church of St. Ruphinus: Sarcophagus of III c., with reliefs of the myth of Diana and Endymion.

Rocca Maggiore

At the summit of the hill that rises above Assisi, stands the Rocca Maggiore, at 505 meters above sea-level.

It is a mediaeval fortress of imposing bulk, bristling with towers and bastions, with mansards and passages. By reason of its structure, so varied, and the movement of the architectural mass, it is to be considered among the most beautiful and important defense works of the Middle Ages.

The first castle was built by Frederick Barbarossa, in 1174, and was destroyed in 1198 by the people of Assisi, who rebelled against the tyranny of the teutonic Duke Conrad of Urslingen. It was rebuilt by the Papal Legate, Cardinal Albornoz in 1367.

The additions, made under various rulers, extended until 1535.

The present plan is trapezoidal, with square towers at the corners and a circular bastion at the entrance.

To the west juts another wall, with a long and atmospheric internal passageway leading to a twelve-sided tower; at the center is the castle keep, containing the living quarters of the castellan.

From the height of the square tower may be seen a vast panorama: to the north the deep, wild gorge of the Tescio; to the east Mount Subasio; to the south the Umbrian plain from Spoleto (which is easily visible on a clear day); at the foot the red roofs of Assisi, from which emerge towers and campaniles, with the Basilica of St. Francis to the right and the Basilica of St. Clare to the left.

Above: *Via Perlici, in the mediaeval quarter of Piazz Nuova.*

Below: *Rocca Maggiore (The Great Fortress) and wall, seen from the little Fortress.*

Right-hand page: *Rocca Maggiore.*

Basilica of St. Clare

We should give a brief sketch of the life of St. Clare, i explanation of the pictures attributed to Cimabu conserved inside the Church. The Basilica of St. Clare, i Italian Gothic style, was built according to a design b the architect Filippo da Campello, in the years from 125 1265. The new Church was added to that of San Giorgi which held the body of St. Francis until its removal to i present location. It should be remembered that th priests of this Church were the first teachers of the youn Francis. The façade is very beautiful, with its decorativ stripes of alternating rose and white, with a port embellished by two symbolic lions, and at the center great rose-window, magnificently wrought. To the le of the façade were added, for the necessary stabilit three flying buttresses, which do not in the least distur the aesthetic balance of the façade; indeed, they increas it. At the height of the apse a soaring pointed belltowe the highest in Assisi, enlivens the architectural move ment of the complex.

Right-hand page: *Basilica of St. Clare: St. Clare and eight episodes from her life: panel attributed to Cimabue, in transept to the right.*

SANCTA CLARA

Basilica of St. Clare: Francis consecrates Clare to God, after cutting off her blonde hair, on the night after Palm Sunday of 1212. (Third square of panel attributed to Cimabue)

Basilica of St. Clare: Bishop Guido gives an olive branch to the young Clare, on Palm Sunday of 1212. (First square of panel attributed to Cimabue).

The interior is in the shape of a Latin cross, with one nave, an in the Gothic style.

Sanctuary: the vault was frescoed by an unknown follower Giotto, with figures of saints and angels. The main altar, uphel by twelve small columns of XIVth century Umbrian work ma ship, is enclosed within a gate of wrought iron, of considerab artistic merit. In the Apse hangs a handsome Crucifix, painte on a carved wooden tablet, by a follower of the painter Giun Pisano. In the left wing of the transept, on the end wall, is painting of the Nativity, of the Umbro-Sienese School of the XI century.

In the left wing of the transept, on the right and left walls at frescoes by Stefano and other Giottesque painters. On the wa to the left hangs a painting attributed to Cimabue, because some distinctive traces of his style: the figure of St. Clare, ven elongated, stylized in expression, and surrounded by eigl symmetrical panel paintings, recounting the principal episode in the life of the Saint.

A BRIEF SKETCH OF THE LIFE OF ST. CLARE, FOLLOWING THE ILLUSTRATIONS OF THE WORK ATTRIBUTED TO CIMABUE

From left to right, beginning at the bottom:

St. Clare was born on the 16th of July of 1194, to the noblema Favarone di Offreduccio and his lady Ortolana. Clare grew u in a cultivated and wealthy household, and she was permitte to learn to read and write in Latin, in contrast to the custom the times that excluded women from even the primary ele ments of learning. Ortolana, a pious woman who had made pilgrimage to the Holy Land (an exceptional thing for the time), took great care in the religious education of her daughte Clare, who distinguished herself among all the other youn girls in the practice of her faith and in her devotions, to the ex tent of putting on a hairshirt at a very early age. When she wa fifteen years old, she refused to marry a noble suitor, because as she explained to her astonished parents, she was consecra ed to God. This private consecration was reinforced in he when she heard the Lenten preachings of Francis in th Church of San Giorgio, in 1212.

First tablet: The Bishop Guido, on Palm Sunday of the above mentioned year, gives an olive branch to Clare, in the Cathedr of San Rufino. The Bishop gestures with particular tendernes toward Clare, since he knows, from Francis, what will happe on the succeeding night.

Second tablet: In the night Clare escapes from her paterna home and, accompanied by her nurse Bona di Guelfuccio, goe to the Porziuncola. Francis and his brothers are waiting for he with lighted torches, on the edge of the wood, and they mee and accompany her to the Church.

Third tablet: Here, Clare, having laid aside her beautifu clothes and jewels, puts on a rough tunic and belts her wais with a cord. Francis cuts off her blonde hair and covers he head with a black veil. She pronounces the vows of povert chastity and obedience, and recognizes Francis as her Superio Thus she initiates the Order of Poor Clares. When the ceremon is finished, Clare is conducted to the Convent of the Bene dictine Nuns of San Paolo near the Insula Romana (toda known as Bastia).

ucifix which spoke to Francis in the little Church of San Damiano (XII c., painted on wood).

Fourth tablet: Her father Offreduccio tries in vain to take Clare away and return her home.

In the face of his daughter's firm determination, he tries to retake her by force from the convent. Clare then clings to the altar, considered a sacred act and so recognized by, law, and the father has to give her up.

Fifth tablet: Agnes, the sister of Clare, on the eve of her marriage, in turn abandons her house and flees to the same convent. The fury of Offreduccio cannot be contained: he goes again to the convent, accompanied this time by armed men. He has no intention of losing another daughter. They take hold of Agnes, with the intention of carrying her home, but they cannot. Through the intercession of Clare's prayers, the body of Agnes becomes as heavy as

lead, and impossible to move. The arm of the father, who threatens to strike her, is paralyzed in the air.

Sixth tablet: St. Clare in the Refectory of San Damiano, in the presence of Pope Gregory IX, blesses the bread before distributing it, whereupon each piece is miraculously marked with a cross.

Seventh tablet: A group of virgins, wearing golden crowns, appear to the dying Clare: the Madonna covers her with a splendid veil.

Eighth tablet: Innocent IV celebrates the funeral of the Saint.

From the wall on the right of the nave one passes to the restored Church of San Giorgio, transversely divided into two parts by a glass partition.

The first part (toward the apse) is called the Chapel of the Sacrament, and it contains frescoes by followers

of Giotto and by Andrea Bologna; the second, the Chapel the Crucified, guards the Cruc that spoke with St. Francis in S Damiano, in 1206, indicating to h his mission: «Go, Francis, and build my house, which as you se falling into ruin». This crucifix v brought from San Damiano to present Motherhouse of the P Clares when they were transfer from the original convent. It was posed to the public, after the resto tion of the Chapel, in 1958.

It is painted on a tablet of carv wood. in Umbro-Romanesque st still somewhat Byzantine.

On the end wall, behind a grate, kept the relics of the Saint.

Descending a staircase, at the cen of the Church, one reaches the cr wherein is kept the casket conta ing her mummified body.

Basilica of St. Clare: Transept on the left - The Virgin Mary u the Infant Jesus (Table in the manner of Cimabue).

Basilica of St. Clare: Nativity scene - fresco of the Umbri Sienese School, in transept to the left.

bbey Church of St. Peter

Romanesque façade, with traces
Gothic influence, lacks a pedi-
nt: it is divided into two sections
cornice of small projecting arch-
In the lower half there is a plain
or, with two column-bearing li-
; in the upper three magnificent
e-windows. The construction of
Church was begun in 1029; the
rk, several times interrupted, was
npleted in 1268.
rior: contains three naves with
e. The sanctuary is crowned by a
racteristic eight-sided cupola of
centric rows of stone. The interi-
dornments and the square pillars
all in stone.
result is a sober and solemn at-
sphere. On the sides of the portal
on the walls of the sanctuary are
bs in the Gothic style.

Outskirts of Assisi: Church of San Damiano

One should not leave Assisi without visiting its outskirts: the Franciscan message is in fact repeated to us with gr[...] sweetness by the enchanting Umbrian landscape, by the low voices of the little sanctuaries brought to life by [...] Francis, and by the lonely hermitages that heard his prayers and witnessed his ecstasy.

CHURCH OF SAN DAMIANO

One reaches it by car, along an asphalt road branching off the road that encircles the city. It is also possible to reac[...] on foot by taking a steep country road.The Church rests on the hillside halfway between Assisi and the plain: i[...] surrounded by the silvery grey of olive groves and a few very high, very dark, pointed cypresses. It is an oasis of q[...] et peace, of almost mystical recollection. Here Francis composed the «Canticle of the Creatures»; here, with the wo[...] of Christ, the Franciscan movement had its beginning. The little rustic Church, dedicated to the Saints Cosmas a[...] Damian, was materially restored in 1207 by St. Francis and some of his first followers. The façade is extremely simp[...] a rose-window without ornamentation and three small windows, one of which illuminated the dormitory of St. Cl[...] and her Sisters. In front of the entrance is a paved brick square, with a rustic portico at its base and three support[...] arches. The masonry of the façade is of small stones and pebbles. The work is surely that of someone far from ex[...] in the art of construction, and very likely Francis himself worked on it: a moving thought.

Church of San Damiano: façade and arcade.

THE INTERIOR

From the portico one descends into the little Church, which has one nave and a small apse. The walls and the ogival vault have been blackened by the centuries. On the right, around a niche which once was a small window, frescoes by an unknown follower of Giotto depict three episodes from the life of the Saint; the prayer in front of the Byzantine Crucifix; the money thrown in through the little window, as an offering for the restoration of the Church by its guardian; the father, Pietro di Bernardone, asking in a threatening way to have his money back.

Again on the right, in a small chapel, hangs a precious wooden Crucifix, by Frate Innocenzo da Palermo (1637), known as the «Crucifix with three expressions», as the face takes on three different attitudes (suffering, agony, death), depending on the side which it is viewed from, left, centre, or right.

At the centre, above the altar, hangs a copy of the Crucifix of St. Damiano, that spoke to St. Francis (we have seen the original in the Church of St. Chiara). In the apse: a small wooden choir, dated 1504; on the wall a decaying fresco from the XI century (Madonna with Child, St. Damiano and St. Rufino). A small side door shows us into the first dwelling of the Poor Clares: in 1212 Francis enlarged the preexisting tiny Convent, and asked Clare and her poor nuns to live there.

SMALL CHOIR OF ST. CLARE

It is a bare room, where the Poor Clares gathered for common prayer and to sing psalms and praise the Lord. This small choir, which includes a rough wooden back, a primitive kneeling-bench, and a simple and unpretentious lectern, symbolizes the poverty and simplicity of holiness.

Interior.

On the left, on the end wall, a niche, where, according to tradition, St. Francis hid to escape his father's rage.

Climbing a steep little staircase, one reaches St. Clare's small garden: a narrow enclosed terrace, with only the Southern side open to the plain. Here the Saint, in her illness, retired to breathe fresh air and to cultivate some flowers in the vases.

A few steps up farther and one arrives at the Oratory of St. Clare: to the left of the apse is the niche which held the ivory Monstrance containing the Holy Sacrament.

On the 22nd of June of 1241, Assisi escaped the sacking of the Saracens under the command of Vitale d'Aversa, by the grace of St. Clare's prayers. Tradition holds that she held up to the invaders the Monstrance with the Sacrament, and that the soldiers and horsemen took flight, unable to bear the brilliance of the light pouring from the Sacred Host. Assisi, on the 22nd of June of each year, celebrates the Feast of the Promise, in memory of the liberation of the city.

Facing the altar of the Oratory, there is a large cupboard containing relics, among them a breviary written by Fra Leone and the little bell of St. Clare.

One passes then into the dormitory of the Poor Clares, where the Saint died on the 2nd of August of 1253, in her sixtieth year. Thence one goes down into a Choir of Franciscan simplicity. From the Cloister one passes to the austere refectory of St. Clare, with its darkened vaults, cointaining the same tables that were there in her time, now battered by the centuries.

Church of San Damiano: Cloister of the convent.

ermitage of the Prisons

uing from the Porta Cappuccini one ascends to the Eremo delle Carceri (the Hermitage of the isons), located in a gorge between Mount Subasio and Mount San Rufino, at 800 meters above a-level. It is an hour's walk, or fifteen minutes by car. In this case the significance of the word risons» is that of a «solitary place».

rancis, after his conversion entered a period of worry and doubt as to what he ought to do: bether to attend solely to his prayer or whether occasionally to preach. Above all he longed to iow the will of God… The divine reply, given through the revelation to San Silvestro and to St. are, was the following: that God had not called him to this state only for himself, but in order at he bear much fruit in the souls of others, and that many should be saved through him».
he Little Flowers of St. Francis - XVI).

ancis obeyed and became an ardent evangelist and missionary; even so, he retained the soul of hermit. In every region he preached in, he sought a solitary retreat for prayer (S. Urbano near rni, Fonte Colombo near Rieti, La Verna in the valley of the Casentino, Le Celle near Cortona, d many others, today each an important step in the Franciscan itinerary.
Assisi his favourite retreat was the Eremo delle Carceri.

Hermitage of the Prisons.

Originally it was a small oratory granted by the Commune of Assisi to the Benedictines of Mount Subasio, and from these it passed to St. Francis. St. Bernardino, in the first half of the fifteenth century, added a small Church and a little cloister.

A centuries-old forest and shady woodland surround the small convent: scattered about it are hidden the grottoes of the hermit saints. The uproar and the anxiety of the world have remained at the edge of the wood: inside one breathes the pure air of Franciscan mysticism.

Along a footpath we arrive at the door of the convent. Inside, we find ourselves before a small cloister with, at its center, a well; to the left, the Convent of San Bernardino; facing it, the entrance to the little oratory, the original nucleus of the hermitage.

The interior is composed of the small Chapel of Santa Maria and a miniscule Choir. Above the altar hangs a pre-Giottesque Crucifixion. A ruined stairway leads to the «Grotto of the Saint». Thereafter we may see the «Devil's Hole» (a vertical split in the rock); a tiny terrace above a deep gorge; an ancient wood reminiscent of the colloquy of the Saint with the birds.

Passing over a bridge, we find to the left a small and very beautiful bronze sculpture by Rossignoli, recalling the episode narrated in the Little Flowers of St. Francis, in Chapter XII.

Hermitage of the Prisons.

Hermitage of the Prisons.
Above left: The Grotto of St. Francis. *Above right:* The old woodland, suggestive of St. Francis' colloquy with the birds.
Below: The little Cloister.

Feasts and traditions of Assisi

Calendimaggio or May-Day is so called because "calendae" meant the first day of a month, according to the Roman calendar. This is, therefore, a feast of pagan origin, though, even on this occasion, people also try to commemorate Francis and his thoughtless youth. It takes place on the last day of April and the first day of May. It is an outburst of joy and freshness, of songs and sounds, of traditional costumes and flowers. It is the celebration and exaltation of Spring that expresses itself in the people and things with the joy of life. This festival is close to the hearts of the people of Assisi who take part in it wearing their traditional costumes. Its aim is the conquest of the "palio" (a symbolic finely decorated banner), disputed between the "upper part" and the "lower part", the two quarters into which the town is divided. The judges award the "palio" to the part that has distinguished itself for its costumes, songs, flagwaving, and in the cross-bow archery competitions.

Among the religious feasts that of the **Pardon of**

isi is quite important. It commemorates the indulgence ained by St. Francis on the occasion of the official approval his Rule from Pope Honorius III, for all those who would go the Portiuncula asking God to forgive their sins. This feast es place from July 31 to August 2, drawing crowds of grims coming from all parts of the world.

her religious feasts take place to commemorate St. Francis' th (October 4) and that of St. Clare (August 12). Other cele- tions are connected with more important feasts, such as ly Week, Ascension Day, Pentecost, Corpus Domini. Particu- y interesting and suggestive are those associated with Holy ek, including processions along the streets of the town with ded friars bearing crosses and the symbols of Christ's sion, and other monks and people bearing torches. They include a re-enactment of the "Deposition from the Cross", r the style of some ancient religious plays.

rth mentioning are also the processions and the rites cele- ed on various days of the month (on Fridays and Sundays) taking place after sunset, when the Franciscan Friars gregate in the Basilica of St. Francis and in the square before order to commemorate the Saint and some episodes of his

ugh such ceremonies and feasts are mainly religious, they almost all characterized also by other features, such as orical and cultural commemorations that give a special rm to them, accompanied as they are by the people who ade wearing their colourful costumes, and by traditional s.

Santa Maria degli Angeli

Descending from Assisi to S. Maria degli Angeli, at about two hundred meters distance, on a levelled tract, we encounter a building called «Casa Gualdi», where Saint Francis, on the eve of his death, stopped the bearers of his stretcher, who were taking him to the Porziuncola, so that he might look back, for the last time, at his native town, and impart to it his blessing.

About the spot where the house is there existed in the twelfth century the hospital of S. Salvatore delle Pareti, where lepers, exiled from the community, were enclosed, being entrusted, for their food and clothing to public charity.

The place, being considered infections, aroused fear and repugnance, and no one dared approach it. The young Francis won here his greatest victory: he kissed the hand of, and embraced a leper, in the name of the Lord.

In his spiritual testament, the following words are written:

The Lord thus gave me, Brother Francis, the grace to begin to do penance: when I was still in my sins, it seemed to me a bitter thing to see the lepers, and the Lord Himself took me among them and I showed them pity: when I left them that which at first appeared bitter to me quickly changed into sweetness in soul and body.

> ### SANTA MARIA DEGLI ANGELI
>
> **This is today an industrial town, spread around its large Basilica, the construction of which began in 1569, on the designs of the Perugian architect Galeazzo Alessi. In 1832 an earthquake caused the vaults to crumble: there remained standing only the cupola and the walls. It was immediately rebuilt. In 1927 the present façade in the late Renaissance style was added by the architect Cesare Bazzani.**

Basilica of Santa Maria degli Angeli

EXTERIOR

The façade has a central body with an entrance surmounted by a loggia. Between the old and the new façade a vestibule or portico, of considerable size was built. On the pinnacle of the dome is placed a statue of the Madonna, in gilded bronze, by G. Colasanti. A magnificent paved esplanade, encircled by tall-trunked trees, symbolizing the old forest of the Porziuncola, lies before the superb façade. On the left side of the Basilica the Medici family had a long fountain built in 1610. Known as the "Twenty-six sponts", it was intended to relieve the crowd wich poured into the city on 2nd August to avail themselves of the Pardon of Assisi. The most interesting architectural view of the Basilica is composed of the complex of apse, cupola and belltower. The elegant dome, with skylights, posed on a polygonal drum, with large windows and cornices, is the work of Galeazzo Alessi. The poet Giosué Carducci mistakenly attributes it to Vignola: this error takes nothing away, however, from the descriptive power of his lines:

Brother Francis, what air embraced this lovely dome of Vignola, where crossing your arms in death, you lay naked and alone upon the ground».

INTERIOR

The plan of the Basilica is of three naves, with transept and apse: it is 150 metres long. and 64 meters wide: few churches in the world are as large.

The solemn atmosphere created by the majestic vaults, by the tall square pillars, by the white, unadorned walls, prepares the soul for the encounter with the most precious treasure of Franciscan spirituality: the size of the building seems almost to dissolve itself before the desire to hurry one's steps to reach the **Cappella della Porziuncola.**

All the architectural lines converge upon the humble little chapel, and exalt it: we must recognize how happily Alessi worked out the theme assigned to him by the commissioners.

Cappella della Porziuncola

The etymology of the name «Porziuncola» can be based on two hypotheses; the first, that it derives from the «small portion» of land upon which the Church was built, pertaining as it did to the then vast patrimony of land belonging to the Benedictines; the second, as a long pious tradition would have it, of a «small portion» of stone, from the tomb of the Madonna, brought by four pilgrims returning from the Holy Land and inserted, as a relic, in the walls. The building of the Chapel goes back to the fourth century: it is known that it passed into the hands of the Benedictines in the Sixth century. It is a modest building of a rectangular shape, with a small apse. The Gothic vault, similar to that of San Damiano, is the result of restoration made by Saint Francis himself. When, in fact, Francis chose it for his use, it had only the outer walls. The Benedictines let it to Saint Francis, for the yearly payment of a basket of fish from the Tescio. Actually the Benedictines wished to give it to him, but Francis, in observance of the principle of absolute poverty, cardinal to his Rule, excluded all ownership, and persuaded the Benedictines to accept a symbolic rental for his occupation. Here he stayed with his first companions for three years, until 1209, when, because of the growing of his followers, he transferred his little community to Rivotorto, into a small house called the «Hovel» (il Tugurio). He returned in 1211 and constituted the firs[t] Franciscan «place»: he used the word «place» ("luogo"), not con[vent], for the word convent bore too much of the suggestion o[f] property and stability. Around the little Church, in the wood[s] sprang up tiny huts of woven branches and mud, without fu[r]nishings of any kind, and only sacks of straw to lie down upon[.] The Porziuncola was the center of gathering for prayer in com[mon] and for the singing of praises to the Lord. Inside this litt[le] Church, on the night of Palm Sunday, on the 18/19 of Marc[h] 1212, the young Clare, having fled from her paternal home[,] made her vows as a nun, initiating the Order of Poor Clares. I[n] 1216, at the Porziuncola, after a vision, Saint Francis obtaine[d] from Christ the grace of a complete pardon for all those who a[f]ter confessing and receiving Communion, visited the littl[e] Church. The indulgence was approved and promulgated b[y] Pope Honorius III, who fixed the dates of 1st and 2nd of Au[gust] of every year. In the Porziuncola all the Chapter meeting[s] of the Brothers were held, to discuss the Rule. This was con[sidered] necessary in order to regulate the continuous flow int[o] the Order of proselytes in Italy and in France, Spain and Ger[many]. The Franciscan movement was assuming such propo[r]tions as to be the subject of no light concern for its Founde[r.] The Chapter of the Stuoie (mattings), in the Spring of 1221, [is] famous as a proof of this expansion: around five thousan[d] monks, representing innumerable small communities scattere[d] over Europe, participated.

EXTERIOR

The façade is decorated by a fresco by G. F. Overberk [of] Lubeck: Saint Francis imploring the Plenary Indulgence. [At] the top of the pediment is a small pointed Gothic structu[re] which, in truth, in accords with the very elementary lines [of] the little Church. At the threshold of the door one reads. Th[is] «place is holy».

INTERIOR

The interior of the little Church is bare and austere: walls [of] unfinished stone; vaults darkened by centuries and nev[er] touched again after the restoration effected by Francis; a st[u]pendous polyptich, on a background of gold, by Ilario [di] Viterbo (1393) representing the Annunciation, at the center [,] episodes from the life of the Saint. Saint Francis, dying, seiz[ed] with love for his Porziuncola, said to the sorrowing mon[ks] standing around him:
«Take care, my dear children, not to leave this place; so that [if] you should be driven away from one part, come back again [to] another, for it is truly holy, and it is a house of God. Here, wh[en] we were few, the Most High made us grow in numbers; here [he] illuminated the hearts of His poor little ones with the light of [His] love; here he who shall pray with devotion shall obtain whate[v]er he asks for, and he who shall desecrate this place shall be t[he] more severely punished. Therefore, my sons, consider th[is] place, this house of God, worthy of honour, and with all you[r] hearts and with voices full of Ioy and praise, here sing to t[he] Lord». (Words of St. Francis dying. Celano, Vita I di S[an] Francesco, pp. II, c. 7).

CAPPELLA DEL TRANSITO

Even while rigidly respecting the poverty of the «luogo» (place), Saint Francis permitted the construction of a small walled cell, to be used as an Infirmary for any monk who fell ill. Here Francis passed the last few days of his life. On the 3rd of October of 1226, feeling that the end was near, he caused himself to be placed, naked, upon the ground.

«Thus laid down in the dust, without even his sackcloth, he raised his face, as always, to the sky but he did not forget to cover the wound in his right side, so that it could not be seen. The companions of the saint wept like men crushed by immense sorrow. One of these, whom the man of God called his Guardian, guessing, through divine inspiration, his great wish, ran quickly to bring his tunic and cord, and offered them to the Poor Little One of Christ with these words: "I am lending these to you, as to a beggar, and you must take them, in holy obedience". Francis was pleased, and felt in his heart the holy happiness of having remained most faithful to Lady Poverty».
(S. Bonaventura, XIV, 4).

After the death of the Saint the little Infirmary became a Chapel. The external wall is covered with a fresco by Domenico Bruschi «The death and funeral of S. Francis». The wooden door is the original one.

INTERIOR

On the walls are frescoes by Spagna (second decade of the sixteenth century), with the figures of Franciscan Saints and of the first companions of the Saint himself. Over the altar is a precious statue in white glazed terracotta, by the famous ceramic sculptor Andrea della Robbia.
In the cupboard, on the right, is a reliquary containing the «belt» used by the Saint.

THE CHOIR AND THE PULPIT

The wood inlays are the work of Franciscan artisans of the seventeenth century.

THE SIDES NAVES

Along the side naves are numerous chapels frescoed by noted painters of the last century, among them Sermei, Pomarancio, Maronelli, Giorgetti and others. We suggest stopping in the fifth Chapel on the right nave, where in the fresco attributed to Pomarancio, «The Procession of the Veil of the Madonna», can be seen a representation of the façade of the Church before the earthquake of 1832. The façade of Alessi is certainly more modest, but more in accord with the architectural design of the whole. From the right arm of the transept one passes to the

SACRISTY

A large room whose walls are lined with great cupboards of inlaid and sculptured wood of the seventeenth century. There is also a painting representing the «Redeemer», of the Umbrian School, but of difficult attribution (Perugino, Gian Nicola di Paolo, G. Manni). To reach the Rose-Garden one passes through a corridor where, in a niche, is placed a statue of Saint Francis holding a nest of doves. Proceeding, one passes a colonnade, built at the end of the last century: to the left one sees a grassy lawn where stands a base of travertine holding the

bronze group «Saint Francis and th Ewe-lamb», by the sculptor Vincenz Rosignoli (1916). Around the base a four low-relief sculptures: Saint Fra cis and the Locust; Saint Francis an the crow; Saint Francis and the nigh ingale; the dying Saint Francis and th larks. The expression of Saint Franc speaking to the Ewe-lamb is full tender sweetness. The monument meant to celebrate the love of Franc for animals. To explain the little mor ument, we reproduce the episoc from which the artist took his inspira tion.

«Another time at Santa Maria del Porziuncola a ewe-lamb was given him. The man of God greatly love her for the innocence and simplici of which she was a symbol.
He exhorted her to praise God and n to disturb the monks. And the lam as though she understood the piety the Saint, obeyed in everything, wit admirable faithfulness» (Sa Bonaventura, VIII, 7).

«At the hermitage of Averna, also falcon, who had a nest there, a tached himself, with singular tame ness, to the man of God. Every nigl with his own voice, he signalled th hour in which the man of God we accustomed to arise for the Divin Offine.
He was therefore much prized l

Francis, because he served to drive away any sleepiness or laziness. But if he happened to feel unwell, the falcon was considerate, and did not call him». (San Bonaventura, VIII, 10). Near the cell of the Saint of God at the Porziuncola a cricket, perched on a fig tree, sang insistently: the blessed Father one day reached out his hand called the cricket to him very sweetly: "my little sister cricket, come to me!". And the cricket, as though endowed with reason, leapt into his hand. He said to her then: "Sing, my sister cricket, and praise with your joyful hymn the Lord your Creator!" The cricket, obedient, began at once to sing, and did not stop until the man of God, who wove his song of praise into hers, told her to return to her usual place». Ibid. CXXX, 172, II).

The larks, who fly in the sunlight and flee from darkness, at the death of the man of God, thought it was night-time, came in great numbers to the roof of the little house, wheeling about in unusual joy, giving lively and happy testimony to the glory of the Saint, by whom they had so often been invited to praise the Lord» (Ibid. XIV, 6).

This love for animals and for all growing things lives today in the hearts of many, reflecting a refinement in the sensibility of man toward nature: it was not so in the time of Saint Francis, when customs were much rougher. We must consider the Saint a precursor, and we should learn from his teachings to safeguard the integrity of Nature, a gift of God. The universality of the sanctity of Francis has his feeling, at its roots as well.

CRYPT

Recent work has brought to light the foundation of the first convent to rise around the Church of the Porziuncola. On the end wall of the new crypt has been placed the polyptich in glazed terracotta by Andrea della Robbia, in six scenes: at the top, Saint Francis receiving the Stigmata, the Coronation of the Virgin, St. Jerome in the cave at Bethlehem; below, in the smaller scenes, the Annunciation, the Nativity, the Adoration of the Magi.

This is one of the most notable works of the master ceramic artist of the fifteenth century, for the fineness of its modelling, for the splendour of the colouring of the glazes, and for the attention to detail.

The Rose-bush

One winter night St. Francis, tempted by the devil, threw himself nude into a thicket: the thorns tore his flesh and his blood reddened the leaves.

By a miracle, the thorns disappeared and the thicket changed into a flowering rose-bush. Such is the tradition! The rose-bush flowers regularly, every Spring: there are no thorns and the leaves are streaked with red. The faithful keep them out of devotion.

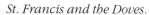

St. Francis and the Doves.
St. Francis and the Ewe-lamb, a bronze group by the sculptor Vincenzo Rosignoli (1912).

CHAPEL OF THE ROSES

The chapel was constructed by St. Bonaventure, Superior-General of the Fran-
ciscans (and biographer of St. Francis), in
the second half of the XIII century, on the
place where the cell of the Saint had been.
The frescoes are by Tiberio di Assisi
(1518) and describe scenes from the life of
St. Francis. Under the Chapel is the Grotto
of the Saint. Beside the statue of St. Francis
in prayer are preserved two beams that
formed part of the pulpit from which was
promulgated the «Pardon of Assisi».

St. Clare.
Grotto of St. Francis.
Chapel of the Tears.

MUSEUM

To visit the Museum one must be accompanied by a monk.

In the first room are kept precious sacred vestments, relics and reliquaries. In the two succeeding rooms, among many paintings, there are three of very great value: the Crucifixion by Giunta Pisano, of 1236; Saint Francis between two Angels, by the «Master of Saint Francis», (in the book the Saint holds in his hands is written: "This tablet was my repose in life and in death"; the portrait of Saint Francis attributed to Cimabue (after the cleaning of the fresco of Cimabue in the Lower Church of the Basilica of Saint Francis, a great resemblance was noted between the two portraits).

Church of Santa Maria di Rivotorto

It takes its name from a winding stream that flows by the sacred «Tugurio», which today is enclosed in a Church of neo-Gothic style.

The Tugurio (hovel), of the twelfth century, is composed of two tiny houses, separated by a small Chapel: it is a symbol of Franciscan poverty.

The «place», as the first biographer, Tommaso da Celano, said: *«so poor that it is uncomfortable to sit or lie down there».*

Because of the restricted space, Francis assigned to each of his eleven companions a place, writing their names on the wall and on the beams.

Their Church was the open sky. The monks had raised a wooden cross in front of the Tugurio, and they prayed around it.

The three years spent at Rivotorto are fundamental in the history of the Franciscan movement: it is the heroic and formative period par excellence. Francis remembered it for the rest of his life with great nostalgia.

Various episodes, making up part of the Franciscan epic, occurred in this place.

Here was dictated the first Rule, orally approved by Innocent III in 1209. And Francis himself praises it in his testament: *« since the Lord had entrusted to me the brothers, no one showed me what I ought to do; but the Most High Himself revealed to me that I ought to live according to the Holy Gospel. And this I did, and this I wrote in a few simple words».*

Left-hand page:
St. Francis between two Angels, by the Master of St. Francis.
Crucifixion by Giunta Pisano.
Portrait of St. Francis attributed to Cimabue.
Madonna and Child (Sano di Piero).
On this page:
S. Maria di Rivotorto.
Church of S. Maria di Rivotorto: the Tugurio.

And those who came to embrace this state of life gave everything to the poor and were content to have only a single tunic patched inside and out... and they were ignorant and subject to everyone... and I worked with my hands and I want to work; and I want all the other monks to do honest work, not in order to receive a price for their labour, but to give a good example, and to discourage sloth. Then when we are given no reward for our work, we will seek the table of the Lord, asking alms from door to door» .

The first family of Rivotorto, living *«in absolute destitution, under hardship, very often without even a piece of bread, contenting themselves with turnips given as alms who supported it all in tranquillity of heart and lightness of spirit... who with fervor followed the example given by their father Francis with the most rigid and watchful rigour»***,** (Tommaso da Celano, chap. XVI), was always regarded by the sons of Francis as the ideal community. On the façade, inside the ogival arch of the pediment, is recounted, in a handsome mosaic, the episode narrated by Tommaso da Celano. (Ch. XVI, 43).

«Thus, finding that at that time would pass by those parts, with great pomp and circumstance, the Emperor Otto, on his way to Rome to receive the crown as Emperor of the land, Francis, who was at the Tugurio with the others, near the street where the entourage was to pass, did not even wish to go out to see him, nor did he permit any of his monks to go, except one who was told to announce firmly to the Emperor that his glory would be short-lived». The prophetic warning of Francis on the frailty of human glory, was borne out by the death of Otto within that year.

Chapel of Satriano

Satriano is situated at the very limit of the mountainous territory of Assisi, where it borders on that of Nocera: it is not easy to arrive at this point, and a visit to it can be made only by those who have several days to spend in Assisi, and who cherish the Franciscan mementoes.

On the right side of the Chapel of Satriano a stone is placed, which reads: «In this place, where once stood the Castle of Satriano, the knights of Assisi who, in the summer of 1226, accompanied back to his native place the dying Saint, paused. The International Franciscan Committee decided to record the 700th anniversary of the event by building this chapel».

Chapel of Satriano.

«It came about that the blessed Francis, very ill and almost at the end of his strength, while he was staying in the convent of Nocera, was called back by the people of Assisi, who sent a solemn embassy to bring him home, rather than leave to others the glory of possessing the body of the man of God.

The soldiers who were escorting him, reaching a miserably poor village called Satriano, feeling, from their hunger and the hour, the need of food, but finding nothing to buy no matter how hard they searched, returned to the blessed Francis and said "You will have to give us alms, since we can find nothing". The Saint answered: "You find nothing because you trust more your flies (he called money 'flies') than you do in God. But" he added "go back to the house you have already visited and offering the people the love of God instead of money, humbly ask alms of them...

The knights, swallowing their pride, went, asking for alms, and obtained, for the love of God. much more than they had with money, since the people vied with each other in generous gifts».

(Tommaso da Celano, Vita Seconda, Chap. XLVII, 77).

Every year, on the 20th of September, in memory of the occasion, young men on horseback retrace the road from Satriano to Assisi, escorting a relic of the Saint.

CANTICLE OF THE CREATURES

All-highest, omnipotent, good Lord,
    to you be praise, glory and honour and every blessing.
    To you alone they are due,
    and no man is worthy to speak your name.
Be praised, my Lord, in all your creatures
    especially Brother Sun who makes daytime.
    and through him you give us light.
    And he is beautiful, radiant with great splendour,
    and he is a sign that tells, All-Highest, of you.
Be praised, my Lord, for sister Moon and the stars
    you formed them in the sky,
    bright and precious and beautiful
Be praised, my Lord, for Brother Wind
    and for the air and the clouds,
    and for fair and every kind of weather,
    by which you give your creatures food.
Be praised, my Lord, for Sister Water
    who is most useful and humble and lovely and chaste.
Be praised, my Lord, for Brother Fire,
    through whom you light up the night for us:
    and he is beautiful and Jolly. and lusty and strong
Be praised, my Lord, for our sister Mother Earth,
    who keeps us, and feeds us,
    and brings forth fruits of many kinds,
    with coloured flowers and plants as well.
Be praised, my Lord, for those who grant pardon for love of you
    and bear with sickness and vexation.
    Blessed are those who bear these things peaceably
    because, All-Highest, they will be granted a crown by you.
Be praised, my Lord, for our sister, Death,
    whom no living man can escape.
    Woe to those who die in mortal sin!
    Blessed are those whom she will find doing your holy will,
    for to them the second death will do no harm.
Bless and praise my Lord, thank him,
    and serve him in all humility.

St. Francis

PLAN OF TOWN

126

PORTA PERLICI

ROCCA
MINORE

ROCCA

DELLA

VIA

VIA DEL COLLE

JOERGENSEN

DELLE ROSE

OBOVE

DI MINERVA

PIAZZA COMUNE

VIA S. GREGORIO

VIA PORTICA

VIA ROCCHI

VIA ORDINE III

MACELLI VECCHI

VIA DEI PRIORI

DEL PURGATORIO

VIA S. ANTONIO

BERNARDO DA QUINTAVALLE

CRISTOFANI

S. MARIA MAGGIORE

PIAZZA VESCOVADO

VIA S. AGNESE

VIA PORTA MOIANO

PORTA MOIANO

VICOLO S. LORENZO

VIA PORTA PERLICI

VIA DEL COMUNE VECCHIO

VIA DEL TORRI

VIA MONTE CAVALLO

PIAZZA S. RUFINO

VIA S. RUFINO

VIA POZZO DELLA MENSA

VIA DOMO DONI

VIA S. GABRIELE

DELL'ADDOLORATA

CORSO MAZZINI

VIA S. CHIARA

S. RUFINO

VIA GALEAZZO ALESSI

VIA SERMEI

BASILICA S. CHIARA

DELLE

FONTI

DI

MOIANO

VIA BORGO ARETINO

VIA DELL' ANFITEATRO

VILLAMENA

VIA EREMO DELLE CARCERI

PORTA CAPPUCCINI

PIAZZA MATTEOTTI

PARCO DEL PINCIO

PORTA NUOVA

LARGO PROPERZIO

PIAZZALE DELLA PALESTRA

VIALE UMBERTO I

S. DAMIANO

RIVOTORTO

S. MASSEO